Rob Versus Humanity

The Last Line Of Defense In Outwitting, Outlasting and Outliving Time Wasters, Fraudsters and Fools.

Rob Anspach

Rob Versus Humanity

The Last Line Of Defense In Outwitting, Outlasting and Outliving Time Wasters, Fraudsters and Fools.

Copyright © 2020 Anspach Media

Cover design by: Freddy Solis

All rights reserved. No part of this book may be reproduced or transmitted in any form or by any means without written permission from the author.

ISBN 13: 978-1-7324682-4-5

Printed in USA

Disclaimer:

Oh yes, we must have a disclaimer…it makes the lawyers happy. The author has spent a lifetime using sarcasm as a means to grow his business. He shares interactions in this book that you may or may not agree with, his actions and communications are contrary to what most customer service gurus teach. But, it works for him and could work for you too, although highly doubtful.

What People Are Saying

"I sat at the kitchen table with my adult daughter and read her half the book. She couldn't stop laughing. I couldn't stop laughing. She kept asking me to continue reading because it was so entertaining and so true. She loved the sarcasm. She loved when the scammers were put in their place. We loved the stories that expose the liars and the time wasters. This book was a quick and fun read in the tradition of all the Rob Versus books. It's enjoyable, it's laugh out loud funny, and you know when you are laughing you've been in his exact situation and wish you had said what Rob had just said. I highly recommend reading Rob's latest book and give it five stars." ~ **Gerry Oginski** – www.oginski-law.com

"Rob Vs Humanity is a really nice book that shows the lighter side of universe. In this book Rob clearly articulates how grown adults do silly things to inadvertently hurt the spirit of humanity for absolutely no gain. There is one BIG difference between Rob Vs Scammers and Rob Vs Humanity. In the Scammers book, the bad guy is TRAINED PROFESSIONAL EVIL who makes deliberate attempts to scam people, rip them off, steal from them. We the society need to understand how scams work so we are not the victims. In Rob Vs Humanity, the bad guy is not evil. The bad guy is us being silly, selfish, un-thoughtful, ungrateful, disrespectful and just nasty. As you read this book, put yourself in the shoes of the 'bad guy'. Have you ever been that guy? Have you ever ruined someone's day? If so, Rob calls you out. So the message of this book is: Don't be that guy. Be nice. Be kind. Be considerate. Be thoughtful. BE A HUMAN. Rob is not against humanity in this book, Rob is FOR humanity."
~ **Parthiv Shah** – www.elaunchers.com

"I live a fairly simple life compared to Rob, and so enjoy him sharing the stories of him "poking the bear" of scammers, morons and liars everywhere!" ~ **Michael E. Schmidlen** – www.digitaldirectleads.com

"Amusing read! If you've ever wanted to respond sarcastically to stupid people yet usually keep your mouth shut, live vicariously through Rob and get this book." ~ **Lynn Swayze** – www.idrm.us

"A quick scan tells me I can't wait to have this book in my hands and in my "Rob Anspach Library"! As always, I love your sarcastic, breezy style!" ~**Ben Gay III**, www.bfg3.com

"Rob Anspach's new book, Rob vs. Humanity, is hilarious! His style may or may not resonate with you, but you can't help but enjoy how he handles the numerous morons in the world around us. Enjoy it yourself and gift a copy to those who need it." ~ **Greg Jameson**, www.webstoresltd.com

"Rob is one of those people who has a lot of depth, experience, and wisdom. But he hides all that under a thick veneer of sarcasm. If you can take a moment and pierce through that sarcasm - you will find many golden nuggets of knowledge. These nuggets will help you grow your business ethically and in a way that will provide an excellent experience to your clients and customers. Moreover, when applied to your personal life, these principles will also help you lead a generally satisfying and happy life. His Rob Vs. series is just a keen observation of the world and what is wrong with it. It is fun, witty, and to-the-point. I learned a lot from Rob." ~ **Manuj Aggarwal**, www.tetranoodle.com

"Someday there will be no more humans...and AI robo-callers will have to taunt and torture each other for eternity. Until then, we have Rob Anspach, the man responsible for causing more smoke to come from peoples' faces than the Marlboro Man and Joe Kool combined. Rob manufactures more triggers than Smith & Wesson. Try to clumsily friend him on LinkedIn or offer him a free cruise without building a relationship first, and you just might end up telling him to F-off in your native tongue. Just know, Rob's books get bigger, badder, bolder and more beautiful each time his phone rings." ~ **Steve Gamlin**, www.motivationalfirewood.com

"In Rob's latest book, Rob versus Humanity", he continues to give his readers actual accounts of exchanges he has with those who would be energized to take advantage or to not give proper help and customer service. Rob says all the things we wish we were quick enough too retort. His continued wit and humor is sure to entertain because therein lies the most vulnerable truths about the deterioration of a servant's heart. Rob has it; we wish everyone did." ~ **Jocelyn Stewart**, www.ucmj-defender.com

Table of Contents

Introduction – Rob Anspach...7

Chapter 1 – Rednecks...9
The Town I Live In..10
A Month Into Covid And This Happens.................................12
My Plans Were Foiled Again...13

Chapter 2 – Time Wasters..15
Kind Sir, I Hope This Text Finds You Well............................16
Oh Yeah, Never Getting That Time Back..............................18
Thank You For Calling XYZ How Can I Help You? 20
I'm Going To Place You On A Brief Hold..............................22
Hey Rob, Since You Are Helping Us.....................................24
Sir, Your Insurance Does Not Cover Out Of Area Service....26

Chapter 3 – Stupid Systems...29
Are You Calling About The Program You Bought & Downloaded?....30
My Love/Hate Relationship With Comcast............................33
Previous Password Cannot Be Used.....................................34

Chapter 4 – Random Idiots...35
This Is Why You Should Never Text Me................................36
Are You The Person In Charge..39

Chapter 5 – My Unfriends...41
Yo, Why Did You Unfriend Me?...42
Can I Get Some Marketing Advice?......................................44
I See You Left My Facebook Group, Can I Ask Why?..........45
Friends In Common, Don't Care!...48
Pfft, I Sound Crazy?...49
See You In Two Years..50

Chapter 6 – Liars...53
Calling Out The Liars...54
I Want To Help You Write A Book..56
Received An Email Asking For My Help................................58

Chapter 7 – Losers………………………………………....61
Why Your Cut & Paste LinkedIn Response Doesn't Work.…...…..62
Five Minutes After Accepting This LinkedIn Connection.…...…..63
I Get This Same LinkedIn Template At Least 10x A Week.…...…..65
Another LinkedIn Loser Gets Called Out……………………….67
So I Receive This Cryptic Email………………………………..69

Chapter 8 – Liv Operator……………………………….71
Those Numbers Are Incorrect……………………………….…72
Why Do We Even Call You?………………………………...…75

Chapter 9 – Cluster Fudged……..……………………….77
It's The AI's Fault………………………………………...….78
Just Sitting Here Minding My Own Business When……..….…..80

Chapter 10 – Getting Cut Loose………..…......…..……..83
The Time When I Fired A Client...……………………….....…84
Are You Going To The Huge Event In California……...….…….87

Chapter 11 – Scammers Galore…………………....…...……91
A Free Top Of The Line Home Security System You Say….....…..92
An Auto Warranty Scammer Called Me……………….……….94
This Is Your Final Courtesy Call…………………………...…..96
Oh Goody The Marriott Travel Scammers Are Calling…..……..98
Speaking Of Hamsters…………………………………...…...100
Discover Card Scammer Called…………………………….…102
Ronnie Johnson Is Calling…..……………………….……..…105
My Buddies From Pakistan Are Calling………...………..……107
Not Alex From Apple…………………………………….……109

Chapter 12 – Living Up To My Title………….…....……..111
Hey Aren't You're the F-You Guy……………………….……112

Chapter 13 – The Power Of Being Me…………….…....……115
What Rob Does Is Not Normal Human Behavior……..…………116

About The Author……………………………………………121

Resources……………………………………………………122

Introduction

What started out as a few posts on social media to help warn people of scams and lousy customer service has morphed into the third book in the Rob Versus series. And like the other books, this one is full of sarcasm, wit and my take on how the world should deal with time wasters, fraudsters and fools.

If, for some unknown reason, you didn't read my other books here's a recap of what the series is all about… I take conversations that happened in real life, online, via text and email and share them to help teach valuable common sense lessons that can benefit everyone.

Well, I would hope that everyone would benefit, unfortunately, as you'll read in this book, many people seem to get triggered very easily and like to throw out the "F" bomb a lot. Don't worry…I've censored that foul four letter word in all of my books. Some may not care, but I do. Hey, kids of all ages read my books. And those kids are society's future leaders.

Now, unless you've been living off planet, or in a secluded cabin off-the-grid with no access to the media then you've had absolutely no clue that humanity went into turmoil during the Covid-19 pandemic. This book, the one you're about to read right now, was born during that chaos. Signs, arrows, masks…the world went full-on nutso and it became the new normal. And there were days were I felt my sarcasm was the only thing keeping society from totally falling apart.

Companies that were delivering awful customer service prior to Corona stepped up their game to provide horrendously worse representation during the lockdowns. It was as if they were all competing in the "Rob Versus" games.

As you'll soon discover I'm not normal. Nor, do I want people to perceive me as normal. I'm not a "yes man". I don't do things so others feel warm and fuzzy inside. Look, I have no time to coddle people.

As an entrepreneur who teaches clients how to build trust, me being my true sarcastic self is that thing they either like or hate. If they like me, great, we become fantastic friends. If they don't like me, that's okay too, but they just don't get to experience my phenomenal service. But they can still read my books if they choose.

Yup, that's just how I roll.

Enjoy the book.

Rob Anspach

www.AnspachMedia.com

Chapter 1

Rednecks

"Because there is no other term of endearment for these folks."

The Town I Live In...

The sign read… "Saterday, AYCE Wings"

So as I drove through the parking lot of the restaurant, I snapped the picture of the sign. I timed the picture so I would capture the sign image as I passed between two cars.

Ironically, when I took the picture the person in one of the vehicles thought I was snapping her license plate and followed me. She approached with "why'd ya take a picture of my license plate?".

Me: I don't even know who you are.

Her: Well, what are you taking pictures of?

Me: The sign.

Her: What sign?

Me: The sign where they spelled Saturday wrong.

Her: Oh, well I'm having a rough week and don't like people taking pics of my car.

Me: Again, I have no clue who you are, but we are in public and your license plate is there for everyone to see.

Her: So you are taking pictures of my plate.

Me: No, again no clue who you are, taking pics of the sign, your car was in the way. Anything else?

{before she sped off, she held up her phone and snapped a picture of me}

Yup, that'll teach me.

Note: Taking pictures of people, places or things while in public is perfectly legal. It may trigger some and you could potentially get into a situation like I did, the best thing to do is remain calm and just explain yourself. Although using sarcasm helps make the situation story-worthy.

A Month Into Covid And This Happened...

I walked outside to the mailbox.

I had no mask on.

Some old fart across street whom I've never met and I don't think even lives there, yells to me, "You need a mask."

I reply, "Why? You're like 100 feet away."

Stranger: It's the law.

So I gave him the universal signal that I don't care.

Stranger: I'm calling the cops.

Me: Tell them to bring masks and some pizza.

{A few hours go by and no cops and sadly no pizza}

And as of the date you're reading this, still no cops... although, I have gotten pizza many times.

Note: Covid turned society into two groups of people... mask wearers and non mask wearers. Ironically, a good portion of mask wearers weren't even wearing them properly. Oh, but heaven forbid if you're caught without a mask on, those improper wearing masked monitors will report you, snap your picture and shame you on social media.

My Plans Were Foiled

Went to the grocery store to buy a few things and decided to get a bottle of Mucinex just in case we need it.

Get to the check out and the cashier wants my ID.

Me: Why do you need my ID?

Cashier: To deter you from making meth.

Me: Huh?

Cashier: You might use the Mucinex in the production of meth.

Me: Not sure how my ID will help you determine if I'm a meth-head.

Cashier: We will know how to find you.

Me: Scanning my grocery card at the beginning of this transaction gives you all my info anyway.

Cashier: I dunno, just following the rules.

So I walk out of the grocery look at my teenage kids and say, "***guess we aren't making meth today.***"

Note: I would rather write books than go full "Breaking Bad"… it's much safer.

Rob Anspach

Chapter 2

Time Wasters

"Hitting your head with a hammer would be more enjoyable."

Kind Sir, I Hope This Text Finds You Well.

Me: I wish it didn't find me at all.

Them: We have heard you are a person of great moral character.

Me: Yes, my greatness is far reaching.

Them: We have a proposition that we think you would find beneficial.

Me: Wow, we don't even know each other and you are already propositioning me.

Them: Our great leader died with a large sum of money and we need your help in transferring those funds to your local bank. To which we will pay you handsomely.

Me: Died you say...with lots of money, hmm.

Them: Yes, and we need your help transferring it.

Me: How much money?

Them: We can't say until you answer some questions.

Me: I can't answer your questions until you tell me how much.

Them: It's a pile of money.

Me: Take a picture of the pile of money so I know you are telling me the truth.

Them: It's an expression.

Me: What is?

Them: There is no pile, we said that so you would know it's a lot.

Me: Well no pile, no deal.

{no reply for 15 minutes}

Them: Sorry we found someone else to help us.

Me: Someone with more moral character than me, that didn't ask you for a picture of the pile of money?

Them: F YOU

{I tried to respond, the number came back blocked}

Note: If it sounds too good to be true… it's probably a scam. Scammers know it's a numbers game, so if they realize they are getting a bit of push back from the people they are trying to scam, they will simply go to the next person. Eventually they will find a victim, let's hope it's not you.

Oh Yeah Never Getting That Time Back

Grr...spent 20 minutes on the phone going through all the prompts

...entering in my account, my zip, my phone number to finally get a live operator who says...

"Sorry our system is down for maintenance, you could try back later tonight or tomorrow".

Me: So why couldn't your automated system tell me that right away instead of wasting 20 minutes of my life?

Them: Well Sir, that would require us to care a little, and since we are working from home fielding annoying calls all day our patience level is at zero.

Me: Sounds like you need a new job.

Them: Sounds like you need to mind your own business.

Me: Aren't we a bit cranky.

Them: Sir, if I was able to access your account I would delete it.

Me: Good thing it's down...because you've given me your name so if my account goes down, so do you.

Them: F-You

{they hung up}

And yes, I took the liberty of sending that conversation to the CEO of the company along with the name given by their phone rep.

Note: Once a customer service representative gets aggressive they need to be fired, immediately. To allow them to threaten customers and go "postal" on their accounts is just wrong. Now before you go all "high and mighty" on me and say "postal" is not a great term to use, well who's writing this book, eh? When you write your book you can use whatever words you like to describe a situation. So don't get all "triggered" man!

Thank You For Calling XYZ Corp How Can I Help You?

Me: Yes extension 5814

Can I get your name?

Me: {I give my name}

Can you spell that?

Me: {Spelling out my name}

Can you go slower?

Me: No, pay attention if you are going to ask someone their name.

I will transfer you, is there anything else I can do for you?

Me: Besides transferring me?

Yes Sir, how else can I help you?

Me: You can order me a vanilla iced coffee.

Sir I can't do that?

Me: Then why did you ask?

Well okay, I will transfer you now.

{15 seconds go by}

Sir, that extension doesn't seem to pick up. Can I help you with something?

Me: I think we already established you can't help me.

Well, okay Sir, do you wish to leave a message?

Me: Not with you, you don't pay attention, and I don't have the time.

{ I hung up }

Note: This is precisely why some companies switched to automating their phone systems… although that's created a whole new set of problems. And as you'll soon discover leads you further down the rabbit hole of horrendous customer service and some nefarious scams.

I'm Going To Place You On A Brief Hold...

You Will Hear Music.

Me: Okay.

{15 mins later}

Hi Sir, you still with me?

Me: Ah, oh hi, yup.

Okay I need to put you back on a brief hold again.

Me: Please don't.
{too late, she already did}
{back to listening to stupid music}
{10 minutes later}

Sir, okay we need to escalate this to a top level representative.

Me: I thought I was dealing with a top level representative.

No Sir, I needed to keep putting you on hold so I could talk to them about your issue.

Me: So I just wasted over 30 minutes on hold for you to be a go between?

Yes Sir, but I am qualified to answer most questions.

Me: Just not mine apparently.

Sir, do you want this resolved?

Me: I don't know, how long will I need to be placed on hold again?

{they hung up}

Note: Brief hold times should not exceed a few minutes. And by a few minutes I mean five at most. Not ten. Not fifteen. Not broken down into multiple hold times where the customer calling is forced to listen until their ears bleed. NO! If after 5 minutes of holding, tell the customer you will investigate and call them back when you have the answer.

Hey Rob Since You Are Helping Us With Our Digital Marketing…

We Want You To Join Our Friday Morning Conference Calls.

Me: When?

Them: Friday!

Me: I got that, what time?

Them: 9 am

Me: What time zone?

Them: PST

Me: No

Them: Yes, that's the time.

Me: Then NO I won't be joining you.

Them: Why not.

Me: Well your 9 am is noon my time.

Them: What? I thought you were in our time zone?

Me: What gave you that impression?

Them: Well you came highly recommended by two people I know who live here.

Me: Not seeing why that has to do with me living in your time zone.

Them: So you can't be on the conference call?

Me: Record it and I'll listen to it later or have your team jump on the call earlier.

Them: How about I make the call at 7am PST which is 10am EST will that work.

Me: Yes.

{proceeds to schedule conference call - day of call wastes 30 minutes making intros and I spoke for maybe 2 minutes - this was worse than being trapped in a group chat - told them no more conference calls...ever. Next time email me the transcript.}

Note: Conference calls can be super productive when used in the right manner, although 99% of them are a total waste of time and could've been simplified into an email.

Now, if you're going to insist that I be on your conference call...
(1) have a clear agenda,
(2) email the intros out before hand,
(3) oh, and this is an important one...only one speaker at a time, all others should be muted.

Sir, Your Insurance Does Not Cover Out Of Area Service.

Me: Okay well you don't seem to cover in-area coverage either.

Sir, that particular coverage is under another company. You need to call XYXY to get authorization.

Me: Look, I called prior to having this appointment scheduled and you made no mention of that other company.

Well, Sir because you didn't use our provider we cannot accept the invoice.

Me: So basically I have insurance that is pointless.

No Sir, you have insurance that enables you to get the care you need through our extended network.

Me: Extended my ass, your insurance coverage is a load of shit.

Sir, you're not understanding how this works are you.

Me: Oh, I see how it works. You take my money every month and when I'm forced to pay out of pocket for something you should cover I get hosed.

Sir, you have service that was not authorized so we cannot reimburse your invoice.

Me: I don't care if you don't reimburse the whole thing, but at least reimburse 50% of it.

No can do Sir, but I would be happy to direct you to our website that has hundreds of questions and answers.

Me: Your website told me to call if I had questions. So, I called. Now you are telling me to go back to the website. You know this is utter BS the way you are treating people don't you.

Well Sir, I would be glad to direct you to an advocate but they will tell you the same thing.

Me: That your insurance is crap.

Sir, many people have our insurance.

Me: Yes, but how many actually get coverage.

Sir, I can't discuss other people's coverage.

Me: Do you have this insurance.

I can't discuss mine or other people's coverage.

Me: I will take that as a NO.

Sir, is there anything else you wish to discuss.

Me: YES.

Are your questions related to your insurance coverage.

Me: SOME

Sir, you're wasting my time.

Me: Seriously, your company wasted my time, money and energy and now my patience dealing with you.

{they hung up}

Note: Nothing is more frustrating than dealing with a person who doesn't care one iota about you or your situation.

"Thou shalt genuinely, sincerely, from the bottom of your heart CARE, actually give a damn, about the person you are hired to serve. THAT is the spirit of the role when you are hired to be a customer SERVICE representative. You can't provide SERVICE when you FAIL TO CARE."
~ Parthiv Shah of eLaunchers.com

I think anyone who wants to be in customer service needs to have Parthiv's Core Value rule duct taped to their forehead…or at least made to write it freehand 100x times until they can recite it frontwards and backwards.

Chapter 3

Stupid Systems

"Grr, some people are dumber than a bag of wet rocks."

Sir Are You Calling About The Program You Bought And Downloaded?

Me: Yes.

Them: Well that is the technical service department to which you should have pressed option 2.

Me: I did press option 2.

Them: No Sir, you pressed option 3.

Me: Look, I know what I pressed, so instead of arguing with me, just connect me over to that department.

Them: Sir, I do not have the ability to do that.

Me: So I just waited on hold for over 25 minutes for you to tell me you can't help me.

Them: Yes Sir, please call our number and press option 2 this time.

Me: So help me...

{Click, they hung up}

{Dialing the number and making sure I press Option 2}

{I swear the same person answered the phone and then transferred me to tech support.}

Tech: Hi Sir, how can I help you?

{Me explaining the problem.}

Tech: Well that shouldn't be happening.

Me: And yet it is.

Tech: Well how about we refund your money?

Me: How is refunding me money going to help fix the program that isn't working?

Tech: Well we will refund you your initial charge, then recharge your card and then it will pull the updated program into your file so you can redownload it.

Me: Sounds stupid, why would someone design a system like that?

Tech: Don't know, but it usually solves the problem.

{So they refunded me the initial purchase, recharged my credit card, and so I downloaded the updated program and it seems to work}

Tech: Anything else I can help you with?

Me: No.

Tech: Would you mind holding for a brief survey?

Me: How brief?

Tech: I was told its brief, never actually took it.

Me: Mmm…

{I get transferred to the survey message}

"Thank you for agreeing to take our brief survey, time to completion is about 5 minutes depending on how you answer."

Me: {hanging up}

Note: Make your policies and procedures as easy to follow as possible. When they are too complicated it's the customer who ends up being punished. Oh, and a survey shouldn't take more than a minute…any more than that and you're wasting customer's time.

My Love/Hate Relationship With Comcast

Comcast: Hi Sir, how can we help you?

Me: My internet speeds have been slow the last few days.

Comcast: Sir, may I ask what modem you are using.

Me: The one you issued.

Comcast: And that is?

Me: I have no idea off the top of my head – doesn't it tell you in my records? I am renting the box from you, so you should have an idea what it is I have.

Comcast: No Sir, I will need to check.

{Me jumping online to my Comcast account – the modem is listed right on my account.}

Comcast: Sir are you sure you rent a modem from us.

Me: Yup, I'm looking at my account and it displays the serial number of the modem I rent from you.

Comcast: Could you share that with me?

Me: Do you have my account open on your computer?

Comcast: No Sir.

Me: Well I think that would be helpful don't you.

Comcast: I'm going to place you on hold while I check.

{And I was disconnected}

{Ten minutes later my internet speeds magically improved}

Then I go to log back into my account…

And it asks me to create a new account…

Then the nightmare continues.

Your Previous Password Cannot Be Used.

Me: Look you dumb POS this the first time I'm creating this new account, I've never used this new password anywhere before.

You have attempted an illegal operation, your account will be locked now. Please contact customer service.

Me: F You

Note: It's days like this one, dealing with these fools, where I dream of that day long ago when Comcast didn't exist. Oh, it was a glorious time.

Chapter 4

Random Idiots

"Oh yes, I'm a big meanie!"

This Is Why You Should Never Text Me

Some fool is texting me to see if I'd be open to an "As-Is" offer on some home an hour away from me that they believe I own.

So I respond: What were you thinking?

Them: Can you tell me about the condition of the house? Any needed repairs? This will help me calculate numbers.

Me: Have you seen it?

Them: Yes, from the outside. I was curious how old the roof is, and the general interior condition.

Me: So you want to offer an "as-is" price but want to know all the details to possibly discount the "as-is" offer. Doesn't seem like a good idea.

Them: Do you wish to sell the house or not.

Me: It's not even my house, but I think it should get the best price.

Them: What do you mean it's not your house.

Me: I don't own it, never lived there and actually had no knowledge of the house prior to your text.

Them: WTF, you wasted my time.

Me: How so?

Them: You could have just said I texted the wrong number

Me: Where's the fun in that?

Them: {tries to call me - I reject the call}

Them: Answer your phone.

Me: No.

Them: Answer your phone.

Me: Why?

Them: I need to talk to you.

Me: Nah.

Them: Answer your phone a-hole.

Me: Nope.

Them: I'm tired of texting you answer the call.

Me: Stop texting me then.

Them: You wasted my time.

Me: Well stop texting me and your time won't be wasted.

Them: I'm reporting you.

Me: Again still wasting your time.

Them: Shut up stop texting me.

Me: If you text me I will respond.

Them: I'm going to report you.

Me: Are your reporting me or just threatening to report me - why not just stop texting me before you have a heart attack.

Them: You're an ass stop texting me.

Me: You know you can block my number and never see my responses.

Them: I don't care, I'm reporting you, stop replying.

Me: So what offer did you want to make on the house.

Them: Stop texting me.

Me: Block me.

{and finally I was blocked}

Note: If a text makes you rage out like that, it's a clear sign you need lessons in anger management. Can you imagine that fool driving on the highway? OMG!

Are You The Person In Charge..

...of making decisions for your company?

{ugh, people stop using this question when doing sales calls - it screams "I'm desperate and need to make a sale"}

Me: That depends on who you ask.

Them: Well, we are a white label media company that can assist you with outbound leads.

Me: Such as?

Them: Email marketing, search engine optimization, pay per click, social media and funnels.

Me: Do you know what we do here at Anspach Media?

Them: The same things we do.

Me: And why would I use your white label services?

Them: Well, we are cheaper.

Me: Being cheaper is not a valid reason...

Them: We are better then.

Me: What's your website?

Them: {Gives website URL}

Me: In the 5 seconds I glanced over your site, I can tell it's not optimized for search, there is no subscriber opt-in mechanism anywhere on the site which means no collecting of emails and zero funnels. Oh, and you have no social media icons on your website, so do you even have a social presence? Now tell me again why you are better.

Them: Wow, you're mean.

Me: Oh, did I offend you? I'm sorry. You really didn't want to speak to the guy who makes the decisions then, who you really wanted to speak to is our Chief Feelings Officer... let me transfer you.

{they hung up}

Note: Look, I understand some companies have no clue how to market themselves and they think trying to subcontract work from other companies is ideal. But, cold calling competitors saying you are cheaper or better or whatever will only waste your time. Learn how to properly market and those competitors will freely come to you.

Chapter 5

My Unfriends

"The list is long and distinguished."

Yo, Why Did You Unfriend Me?

{message I received through FB chat}

Me: Why does it matter?

Them: Well, we have been Facebook friends for years.

Me: And in all that time this is the first chat message you sent me.

Them: What's that's supposed to mean?

Me: If you were concerned at all about being a friend you could have sent me a message long ago.

Them: Well, I didn't know you would unfriend me.

Me: So you are one of those.

Them: One of those what?

Me: Someone who monitors their friends list so close you know exactly who unfriended you, then you reach out and say "Yo, why did you unfriend me?" Just seems silly to me.

Them: Silly? I don't think it's silly at all. I want to know who my friends are and if they unfriended me I want to know why?

Me: Again...silly. And, honestly I'm glad I unfriended you. I shouldn't have to give a reason why I unfriend social media followers whom I've never interacted with, have not conducted business with or seem to be mentally unstable.

Them: Unstable? F' You!

{and he blocked me}

Note: There are many programs out there that will tell you when a fan has unfriended you. If you wish to know the exact moment they ceased being friends that's up to you, but my philosophy is to just let them go. It's not really worth the drama to know why or to ask them to be friends again.

Can I Get Some Marketing Advice?

{was the message I received via Facebook chat}

Me: Sure, when do wish to schedule an appointment?

Them: Now of course.

Me: Okay, how will you be paying?

Them: What?

Me: Did you think I was just going to give you advice for free?

Them: Yes.

Me: Do you charge for consultations?

Them: Yes.

Me: So why can you, but I can't?

Them: Well I'm asking for advice not a consultation.

Me: Go away.

Them: What? That's rude!

Me: What's rude is you value your service yet don't value others.

{and he ended the chat, then unfriended and blocked me}

I See You Left My Facebook Group, Can I Ask Why?

{chat message I received}

Me: I'm self-isolating.

Them: What?

Me: I'm social-distancing myself from your group.

Them: What?

Me: You keep using that word.

Them: Sorry, I'm not understanding why you left.

Me: Does it really matter?

Them: Yes, it does.

Me: Why?

Them: Well I need to know if it was something I did, something someone else did or you just don't find the group beneficial anymore.

Me: Yes.

Them: To which part?

Me: All of it.

Them: I don't understand.

Me: And that's why I left, plus you seem needy.

Them: What?

Me: There you go with that word again.

Them: Since you left my group we can't be friends now.

Me: Okay, works for me.

Them: Don't you care?

Me: No not really, go away.

Them: But we have been Facebook friends for a long time.

Me: Apparently not anymore.

Them: I just don't understand any of this.

Me: Okay, let me summarize... I left your group, you questioned me on leaving your group, then said we are no longer Facebook friends, I said fine, and now you are questioning your actions.

Them: No, I'm questioning yours.

Me: So you did understand what was going on?

Them: Fine go, I give you permission to leave my group.

Me: Well thank you Your Royal Highness

Them: F-You

{then he blocked me}

Note: If you are like me, you've probably been added to (or maybe you willingly joined) many groups on Facebook. After a while all that content bogs down your feed and starts to be more noise than one can bare. Removing yourself from groups is a great way to restore balance to your mind.

Now if you're anything like me (which I hope you are not), joining groups and sometimes quitting them is not based on any grounded science or some made up rule. I know you were hoping for some cosmic wisdom here, but there so many different social media groups that to tell you which ones to join really comes down to your sparkling personality. Simply, does it resonant with you? Maybe it did at first, then it didn't, so you leave.

Hey that's life, right? Well, yes, it is!

But if you think you might like to be part of my groups, here they are… and if you quit, I'm not chasing after you, just saying.

The Business Dojo
https://www.facebook.com/groups/thebusinessdojo/

I Love Referrals
https://www.facebook.com/groups/ILoveReferrals/

Rob Anspach's E-Heroes
https://www.facebook.com/groups/eheroespodcast/

Friends In Common, Don't Care!

So I looked at this person's profile.

Something seemed odd.

But we had 103 friends in common.

So I accepted.

When I checked Facebook the next morning...

This person had posted several long winded responses to my posts,

And

Sent me a direct message saying how wrong I was and listed about 15 resources from what looked like conspiracy sites.

I immediately unfriended and blocked the person.

Note: It doesn't matter how many friends in common you have...if your gut is telling you something is odd about a friend request, listen to it. Don't accept.

Pfft, I Sound Crazy?

Hi Rob, nice to connect with you. I would like to offer my services to help you write your first book.

Me: Okay, do you have a DeLorean?

Them: I don't follow.

Me: Well I wrote my first book in 2013 and so if you want to help, you will need a time machine.

Them: That's ridiculous.

Me: Well, do you have another way to get to 2013? Maybe a spaceship to slingshot around the sun or the use of a Stargate during a solar flare?

Them: You sound crazy.

Me: That's debatable...but what's really crazy is you not looking at my profile to see if I've written a book. And had you actually looked at my profile you would see I'm currently producing books 26, 27 and 28. So who's the crazy one now?

{I guess I will never know their answer as they unfriended and blocked me.}

Note: Before pitching someone on your services, look at their profile first… trust me…it's a time saver.

See You In Two Years

Got a friend request from someone that unfriended me two years ago. So knowing full well what would happen if I accepted... I said heck yeah.

{5 minutes later received a chat message with an invitation to their stupid opportunity of the month}

Me: Wow, a whole 5 minutes went by since I accepted your friend request and you're spamming me, I feel so honored.

Them: Is that sarcasm?

Me: No, it's a pile of shit.

Them: What shit?

Me: Your message.

Them: What about it?

Me: Two years ago you unfriended me because I was snarky with your spam message you sent me when I accepted your friend request, now you are spamming me again. Didn't you learn anything in two years.

Them: Yeah, your a jerk.

Me: It's you're, not your.

Them: Don't care, goodbye.

Me: So see you in 2 years, so we can play this game again.

Them: F-You.

{then they unfriended and blocked me}

Note: You would think with all these people unfriending me my friends list would be small. Ironically that's not that case and I'm constantly hitting Facebook's 5000 friend limit. These "unfriends" remove themselves from my list so I can make room for better friends. Aren't they so considerate that way? I think so. Yup, I like when the trash takes itself out.

Chapter 6

Liars

"Liar, liar pants on fire…if only!"

Calling Out The Lies

Hello Rob,

I recently was on the Anspach Media's website and I'm seeing a lot of potential with what you guys can do.

One of our clients is a public speaker and we've helped him rank higher on Google and grow a HUGE social media following which has enabled him to leverage to get a ton more coaching clients and speaking engagements.

We'd love to do the same for you.

Let me know when you are available for a quick call?

Sarah H.

{using a Gmail account and listing the name of the so-called company she works for with address, but no phone or website}

My response:

"You say you went to my Anspach Media website, yet you are emailing me using an email which is not on that website. So most likely you scraped that email off of LinkedIn.

And evidently you have zero clue what we do, so NO I don't think you can help me. Oh but by the way, I took the liberty of looking at your website and the SEO is horrible, no wonder you have to result in spamming people with misleading messages."

{27 minutes later}

Received an identical email from David S from the same company.

I reply:

"David, tell Sarah to stop letting you copy messages, you need to learn how to send better emails, hers was crap and now because you copied, yours is crap too."

{10 minutes later receive message from Sarah}

"F-You"

Note: When you get identical spam messages from different unknown people… it's a scam.

"I Want To Help You Write Your Book."

{was the headline of the email I received}

The email went on and on, and on some more about how they could help me write my very first book. So I looked the email sender up on Amazon to see which books he had authored.

Hmm, not there. I look again. Nothing. So I perused several other author sites...still nothing.

Yet, he wants to help me write my first book. Curious.

So I called the number. The guy answered and sounded so excited someone responded to his email.

I asked him if he knew who I was. He replies, "No" but I could hear him typing away when I gave him my name.

There was a brief pause.

His excited voiced changed to one of disappointment and he asks, "why are you calling me?"

Me: Apparently you Google'd me or looked me up on Amazon.

The Guy: Yeah, you've written many, many books.

Me: That's right and you've written how many.

The Guy: Well none per se, but have helped many get their books published.

Me: How many?

{he hung up - guess he got tired of the call}

Note: If you need help writing a book hire someone who has actually authored and produced many books. It may sound like common sense, unfortunately many take advice from the wrong people who have absolutely zero experience in helping anyone.

Received An Email Asking For My Help.

The person said she received my name as a referral from a friend. Although she couldn't recall friends name. (Red Flag #1)

In her email her firm was looking for a social media manager. But only her name and phone number were listed on the email. (Red Flag #2)

So I emailed back asking for more information and that I would like to see some of their social media accounts and her website URL.

She responded with links to their Facebook and Twitter pages but no website. (Red Flag #3)

Well, I looked at the Facebook and Twitter pages and something struck me as odd. Although there was content on an almost daily basis it seemed that the tone of the posts changed every 30 days or so. (Red Flag #4)

So this time instead of emailing, I decided to call. It went straight to voicemail. So I left a message. Ten minutes later this person called back. Very noisy background as if in a call center. (Red Flag #5)

The person explained that although I came highly recommended they would need ideas, samples and a 30 day itinerary of posts created so they could test them. (Red Flag #6)

I say sure I can do that... for a price.

She informed me that's not how they work. And if I wanted to have lots of success with them and be their social media manager I would need to supply the necessary content to them in the next few days. (Red Flag #7)

I replied...you evidently have no idea who I am.

But here's what I would like to share with you...
(1) I don't do free,
(2) I doubt you will ever hire anyone
(3) You evidently are trying to get free content
(4) You enjoy tricking people
(5) You will continue to do this after I hang up.
{she hung up before I could say anything else}

So when you get emails (or texts, or voicemails, etc.) look them over very carefully...not everyone out there is honest, ethical or cares about you. Unfortunately they only need to convince a few people and sadly they will find them.

My hope is that it won't be you.

Rob Anspach

Chapter 7

Losers

"I almost feel sorry for these people...almost."

Why Your Cut & Paste LinkedIn Response Doesn't Work

"Rob,

It looks like we are connected with some of the same people.

Your background is impressive, I was compelled to reach out. I connect and engage with Health and Network Coaches and would like to add you as a connection.

George"

MY REPLY TO GEORGE...
"Well George here's how you failed...

Compelled? As if some mystic force reached out and took control of you so that you could connect with a total stranger who is connected with some of the same people you probably don't know either.

And you want to connect and engage with Health and Network Coaches well lah-di-dah... I'm in fact none of them. So your connection request is denied."

~Rob

Note: Stop using outdated cut and paste strategies to build a network that doesn't match the people you are actually looking to help.

Five Minutes After Accepting This LinkedIn Connection I Receive...

Hi Rob,

In this message, I am going to share with you some important news. My hope is that this message will provide value to you and your teams. First of all, please allow me to wish you a fantastic 2020 which has got off to a great start. I would say that wouldn't I because for me 2020 is the beginning of my great project!

I have spent more than 30 years working as a facilitator, coach and conference speaker, and I have met and worked with over 65% of the CEO's and leaders of the CAC 40, and together with breath and vocal coach (some unknown person), we are launching « Transformational Leader »

(lists some weblink)

To help today's leaders succeed their transformations by engaging their teams and galvanizing the collective intelligence of their eco-systems. This is our way of changing the world for the better. In order to help thousands of people, we need your help: I have prepared a quick survey to finetune our communication. To thank you for your participation, I've organized a little gift for you. I'm going to send you a short and dynamic video on "Storytelling : the 6 stories all leaders must know how to tell". In fact, it's one of the modules of my online training course "High Impact Presenting". Click here to answer my 5 questions :

=> (another weblink)

Thank you so much for your help. If you have any questions and you'd like to strike up a conversation around these themes, you can contact me.

Warmly, Paul

MY REPLY...

So the very first communication you send after connecting is a spammy message asking me to click some link. Nope. That's not how it works. The correct way is "Hi, thanks for connecting, I took the liberty of looking at your profile to learn more about you, good stuff by the way. If there is anything I can do to help move your business faster send me a chat". That's it. Keep it simple.

Note: LinkedIn can be a powerful social media platform when used correctly. Unfortunately, most use it to spam their marketing messages to anyone regardless if they are an ideal client or not. Remember keeping it simple is better at creating a meaningful relation with a new connection.

I Get This Same LinkedIn Template At Least 10x A Week...

I'm looking to build my network, and came across your profile. I'm a (your industry) with over (some number) years of experience specializing in (what your niche is) for both personal and business clientele. We have a few common connections, and I thought that there could be an opportunity to work together at some point.

Let's break it down shall we...
"***I'm looking to build my network***" really means I want as many people following me as humanly possible.

"***and came across your profile***" means LinkedIn suggested my name and you clicked on the button to connect, you never even took the time to actually look at my profile.

"***I'm a (whatever) with over X amount of years of experience***" - doesn't really mean anything in today's world, heck, you could have gained all your experience the first year and learned nothing since. So all those years of experience mean diddly.

"***specializing in personal and business***" - just means you aren't picky and will accept anyone who breathes as a customer.

"***We have a few common connections***" - means that LinkedIn told them that, they really didn't even look to see, nor did they ask any of those common connections if I'm a good guy, they just clicked the button to connect and hoped I'd accept.

"and I thought that there could be an opportunity to work together at some point" - yeah right, "*could be*" is the keyword word...they should just come right out and bloody well say, "*there is absolutely no chance in hell we will ever work together, but hey there's always hope*".

Note: Stop using this overused template, and start learning how to effectively connect using LinkedIn.

Another LinkedIn Loser Gets Called Out...

Starts out all innocent usually with this tired script...

"Hi Rob, I'm looking to expand my LinkedIn network with other professionals. Would you be open to connecting? Thanks in advance" ~ Belinda"

Then I accept Belinda's connection and within seconds I get some cut and paste pitch wondering what I do and how they can help me.

"Hi Rob, Thanks for connecting. I'd love to find out more about you and some of the things you're working on, so let me know if you're open to a conversation. One thing I did want to share with you real quick which could be really valuable for you is a Sales Blueprint Creator I've been working on. It's FREE, doesn't require you to opt in and will take 2-4 minutes for you to complete. It'll ask you a few questions to get a basic understanding of your business and what's currently working for you before helping you design a complete multistep, multimedia Lead Generation and Sales Process which is tailored specifically for your business. Check it out, have some fun with it and I'd love any feedback you may have or happy to answer any questions it may create as far as how to make things work better for you. Here's the link XXXXX Anyway, I'm always totally respectful of your time and privacy so if I'm stepping over any boundaries and even slightly inappropriate with reaching out feel free to reply

with a hard NO and it'll never happen again. Have a great day, talk soon." ~ Belinda

And as much as I want to respond with "*Read my f-ing profile and learn to use LinkedIn properly you f-ing plonker*". I realize it's not Belinda's fault as she is just following some guru's stupid script. It's sad really, Belinda along with thousands of others have been duped into believing that this method of spamming connections is totally fine and acceptable.

It's NOT!

Stop doing it.

Note: Learn to read people's profiles first. Once you understand what they do then you can simply say, "*Hi, thanks for the connection, I took the liberty of looking at your profile, great stuff, how can I help you succeed faster?*" That's it, that's all you have to do. It's that easy. No long ass worthless scripts. Keep it simple.

So I Receive This Cryptic Email...

{anyone want to guess what they do}

We Want To Give Back
As a simple Thank You for being such a blessing on our lives we want to offer you our June special.
When you get 5 services in office, we will be offering a discount on your 6th!!!
Please call or E-Mail our office to learn more and schedule your next appointment!!

Anyway...after tracing the email, I discovered...
(1) I'm not now nor have I ever been a client
(2) The organization is over 500 miles away
(3) I don't recall ever subscribing
(4) The owner of said business is a LinkedIn connection

Ding, ding, ding...yup, my email was scraped from LinkedIn and tossed into their subscriber list.

Note: Just because you accept someone on LinkedIn does not mean you are granting them permission to add your email to their list. Yet, until LinkedIn changes the way their system works, people will continue to scrape emails from LinkedIn and spam people with their cryptic messages. Ugh.

Rob Anspach

Chapter 8

Liv Operator

"Nope, nothing like a smooth operator."

Those Numbers Are Incorrect!

To Get A Lower Rate Press 1 For A Liv Operator

{I was curious as to what a "liv" operator was so I pressed 1}

{apparently a "liv" operator is code for a thick accented foreign dude who doesn't take kindly to having his time wasted}

Me: Hello.

Liv Operator: Sir I see you pressed 1 to lower your interest rate is that correct.

Me: Sure.

Liv Operator: What's the card with the highest balance - is it a Visa or Mastercard?

Me: No idea.

Liv Operator: Sir I see you make payments every month on time for the last six months and sometimes you make more than your minimum payment is that right?

Me: So you can see about my payment history but have no idea what the card with the highest balance is.

Liv Operator: Sir that is correct can you share that information with me?

Me: Okay I'll play along.
{thought for sure he would hang up, but he stuck with me}

Liv Operator: Can you share with me the card starting with 5.

Me: Five? What five? This card starts with a 4?

Liv Operator: Sir I want your Mastercard number starting with 5.

Me: No can do - I have a Visa and it starts with a 4.

Liv Operator: Okay read those numbers to me.

Me: {I make up 16 digits}

Liv Operator: Sir those numbers are incorrect.

Me: What do you mean they are incorrect...

{I repeat the same 16 numbers I made up prior}

Liv Operator: Sir that number is not correct. Who issued that card?

Me: US Bank.

Liv Operator: No Sir.

Me: Are you calling me a liar? I have the card in front of me.

Liv Operator: Sir, I don't believe you.

Me: That's okay, I don't believe you work for Visa Mastercard either, you stupid scammer.

Liv Operator: You wasted my time you a-hole.

Me: Bwahahahaha.

{he tried to hang up, I stayed on the line laughing, he picked up the phone to hear me laughing - finally the call disconnected}

Note: Most people would just hang up when getting these calls…then again most people don't write books about these calls either.

Why Do We Even Call You?

Press 1 To Speak To A Liv Person.

{Me pressing 1}

Scammer: Sir did you press 1 to get a lower interest rate.

Me: Are you a liv person?

Scammer: Excuse me Sir.

Me: Well your voice prompt system said to press 1 for a liv person, is that you?

Scammer: It's not a liv person it's a live person.

Me: Why did she say "Liv"?

Scammer: F-You.

Me: Bwahahaha

Scammer: Oh it's you.

Me: Darn skippy, and thanks for entertaining me.

Scammer: I don't know why we even call you.

Me: Oh come on, you know you like me wasting your time. It's the highlight of your day.

Scammer: F-You

{he hung up}

Note: Most of these scammers use automated dialers with integrated artificial intelligence that most of the time can't pronounce words correctly. So common words like "Live" are pronounced "Liv". So, you can either hang up or do like I do and completely waste the callers time.

Chapter 9

Cluster Fudged

"And a large iced mocha, please."

It's The AI's Fault

Thank you Google for the most asinine, patronizing, totally non-sensical, cluster fudge of a phone call one can have with your call center.

Called to resolve why 41 of my client's reviews suddenly vanished and the answers they gave were beyond stupid.

Google Rep: The AI algorithm now determines what is and isn't a good review.

Me: So we are at the mercy of a free thinking computer.

Google Rep: The reviews might have been received too close together.

Me: What is the time frame that determines how close reviews should come in?

Google Rep: The person leaving a review is doing so for the first time so it raises a red flag.

Me: Yet, Google encourages us to ask clients to leave a review.

Google Rep: Certain words which go against our community standards might trigger the algorithm and be removed.

Me: And yet, we have no idea what those words are.

Google Rep: The system hasn't caught up yet, so check back in a few days.

Me: Caught up? These were reviews that just vanished. This is a not a game of catch-up, it's a game of the system being too lazy to do its job.

Google Rep: The system is location based so if a review came in outside the service area of the business it won't be recognized.

Me: These were reviews all in the same service area and every single one was a customer. So this statement is invalid like the rest.

So after I countered every excuse they could muster...they simply said "check back in a few days, maybe it'll fix itself."

Yeah, maybe.

But I doubt it.

Note: Google, along with many other companies, used the pandemic as an excuse to close their call centers and have their employees work from home with no oversight. Meaning, those call takers could say and do whatever they wanted and the customer just had to accept it. To me that's not acceptable and I will, when calling, hold them accountable. You should too.

Just Sitting Here Minding My Own Business When...

...my phone rings...

...it's Card Services trying to offer me a lower rate.

Well you know me...

I just had to play along.

Caller: I see you pressed 1 for a lower rate.

Me: You know it.

Caller: May I inquire the card with the highest balance?

Me: Sure.

Caller: Sir?

Me: Yes.

Caller: What is that card?

Me: What are the choices?

Caller: Choices Sir?

Me: Yes, which cards?

Caller: Visa, Mastercard.

Me: Oh okay, I have those.

Caller: Can you read the numbers to one of them.

{Me grabbing an expired Starbucks Visa gift card, reading off the numbers}

{The caller scrambling to enter the numbers into his computer}

Caller: Sir, are you sure this is your highest balance card.

Me: Yup, why?

Caller: Sir, there doesn't seem to be a balance on this card.

Me: Well I did just use it to buy this iced mocha I'm drinking right now.

Caller: A what?

Me: You know a coffee. You can get them just about anywhere. I prefer Dunkin Donuts myself, but the card I gave you I used at Starbucks. Do you want one? I can get you a prepaid gift card while I'm here. I'll need your address to ship the card.

Caller: Do you enjoy wasting our time?

Me: Why yes, yes I do.

Caller: F' you mother f'er

Note: Any time someone calls saying they are Card Services I make it my mission to waste their time.

Rob Anspach

Chapter 10

Getting Cut Loose

"It's what happens when you don't respect me."

That Time When I Fired A Client.

I shared my thoughts about this particular scenario to Facebook. The majority of people who commented sided with my position.

However there was a few who said, "Rob a phone conversation would have simplified this whole matter and you probably wouldn't have had to fire them".

Maybe! But, I highly doubt it.

You see this particular client had been yo-yo'ing us for months. They would say, "Hey send me an invoice and we can get started." So I send an invoice. Then I would wait. Then I received, "I'm moving into a new place, can we wait a month or two?" So we cancel the invoice. Then it was, "Hey I got my tax refund so I have money now, can you send that invoice?" So we send the invoice. Then wait. Then we get, "Sorry was stressed so I took a vacation and spent the money." So I cancelled the invoice once again.

After the second invoice cancellation I should have fired them. But I didn't that's on me.

Well, opportunity presented itself once again, and boy was I ready.

They said this time they were really ready and to send the invoice via email and to text the next day to confirm you sent it.

So I texted as requested a day later. "Sent the invoice."

They reply, "Okay, I'm headed to the mountains...trying to figure out if I am staying here or leaving."

So I replied, "Not sure what that has to do with the invoice."

At this point I kind of knew we would be repeating the whole cancellation thing once again, but really wasn't expecting the client to be rude and disrespectful.

I receive, "Because I'm not near a computer right now that's why, and I really don't need you or anyone else being a dick to me!!!!!"

Maybe it was the 5 exclamations that she typed or the calling me a dick that did it, but honestly the yo-yo'ing was stopping right then and there and she had to go as a client.

So I texted back, "You're fired."

Then I get back not even 2 seconds later, "Fine, I don't care."

And for those that say "Rob a phone conversation...blah, blah, blah", you can run your business however you want...

But one thing I will not tolerate is any client disrespecting me or any member of my team. And when that happens, regardless on the phone, via email or in a text or chat, they will get instantly fired. No exceptions.

I give clients chances all the time...need a few extra days to pay your invoice, just let me know. Need a month to come up with money to get started, sure I'll be here when you want to get started. But disrespect me or my team in any way, shape or form and you're gone, simple as that.

No I will not waste my time trying to win back a disrespectful customer.

Why? Because they will just do it again. Like I said, I give people chances, but when they can't show respect, they need to be cut loose.

Note: Even when you do your due diligence in screening potential customers, there is always a chance some Negative Nancy or Debbie Downer will squeak through. The moment they disrespect you is the moment they should be fired. If you keep them as a client, they will continue to disrespect you and your team making your life miserable.

Are You Going To The Huge Event In California?

{was the question that popped up on my Facebook messenger from someone who bought a few of my books years ago but I haven't really communicated with since}

Me: How many people will be there?

Them: I dunno maybe 10,000.

Me: Good gawd man, no way. That's 9,990 more people than I typically see in a day.

Them: Yeah but (drops the name of some influencer) is going.

Me: Who?

Them: You know that YouTube celebrity that makes all those videos.

Me: Nope, doesn't ring a bell.

Them: Come on, you're pulling my leg, everyone knows who that person is.

Me: I don't get out much.

Them: Well (drops some more names) are going.

Me: Okay and?

Them: Well you should be there.

Me: Why?

Them: You would gain a lot of business.

Me: I already have a lot of business.

Them: You would gain more.

Me: How much more?

Them: I don't know a lot more.

Me: Be specific.

Them: So you want me to throw out a number

Me: Yes.

Them: A lot.

Me: Then no, not going.

Them: Why? You will meet people and gain a lot of business.

Me: Yeah, I think this convo is over.

Them: Well, I'm going to the event.

Me: Why didn't you lead with that?

Them: So you're going?

Me: Nope.

Them: But you said...

Me: Had you lead with that I could have said NO quicker and ended this conversation long ago.

{and I was magically unfriended and blocked}

Note: In my opinion when events are that big, those attending are overwhelmed. For me personally I like attending smaller events where I get to know everyone.

Rob Anspach

Chapter 11

Scams Galore

"If I had a dollar for every time they called...I'd be rich."

A Free Top Of The Line Home Security System, You Say.

Yes Sir, we are giving away a top of the line home security system by GE to homeowners in your area just to try us out.

Me: What kind of system is it?

Them: Again Sir, top of the line.

Me: Yes you said that several times now…what model, what are the features, who monitors it?

Them: Sir it's made by GE, it has so many features that I would need more time to explain them to you.

Me: Hey I answered the phone, I have time…tell me all about it.

Them: Sir, do you have any other questions?

Me: You said you are giving away the system to homeowners in my area, what area would that be exactly?

Them: Sir, the local area around where you live.

Me: And that would be?

Them: Sir are you playing games with me?

Me: Of course, it's what I do.

Them: I hate you.

{and the caller hung up}

Note: These types of calls are a scam. The caller offers something of value in exchange for your address, credit card number or identification. Do NOT ever give out your information to strangers via the phone, email or text. The reason I answer the phone is to waste their time and keep them on the phone so they aren't potentially ripping others off. Of course, then I share my phone adventures with YOU in my books. So if you haven't read, *"Rob Versus The Scammers"* or *"Rob Versus The Morons"* yet, get crackin'…order them from Amazon right now.

An Auto Warranty Scammer Called Me...

Them: Hi Sir, what is the make and model of your vehicle?

Me: 2006 Saturn Rocket.

Them: A Saturn, is that correct?

Me: Yup, a Saturn Rocket.

Them: How many miles are on your Saturn?

Me: Oh about a million miles.

Them: Are you sure about the miles?

Me: Oh yes, it been to space.

Them: It's been where.

Me: Into space.

Them: I don't understand.

Me: It's a rocket it goes into space, around the globe, it goes like 6100 miles per hour.

Them: I don't need to know how fast it goes.

Me: Okay then.

Them: So it's a Saturn then.

Me: Yes.

Them: Okay I think you qualify for our warranty program.

Me: Wow, that's cool. I should tell NASA to call you guys they have hundreds of Saturn Rockets that need warranties.

Them: What? {5 second pause} You just f-ing wasted my time you F-er.

{they hung up}

Note: I love it when a scammer tells me I'm wasting their time when that is exactly what they are doing every time they call.

Here's three reasons you should never give your information to a person calling offering you an auto warranty...
1. They ask for the make and model of your car.
2. They ask for your address.
3. They ask for your credit card information.

When you share all those details, the scammers know where you live and if you have a particular car of interest they now know where to find it to steal it. They also have your credit card information to rack up charges.

This Is Your Final Courtesy Call...

press 1 to get a lower interest rate on your credit card now.

{me pressing 1}

Me: Hellooooo.

Caller (with a thick foreign accent): Hi this is Zack Henderson with the top Visa / MasterCard office.

Me: I'm sorry, you are who?

Caller: Zack Henderson.

Me: Of the Pakistani Hendersons?

{the guy stayed on script and ignored me}

Caller: Which of your credit cards has the highest interest rate?

Me: No idea...but it should be in my records, why don't you tell me?

Caller: Sir, I have no idea, that's why we are calling you.

Me: Wow, so you are from the top office of Visa Mastercard and you have no freaking clue what my interest rate is.

Caller: Do you want a lower interest or not?

Me: How can you give me a lower interest rate if you don't know what my current rate is?

Caller: Sir, that's not how it works.

Me: Well here in America that's exactly how it works son, but I'm sure in Pakistan nobody has a clue.

Caller: F-You.

Me: So is your company going to give me another final courtesy call tomorrow?

Caller: We might call you again two more times today.

Me: I'll be waiting.

Caller: F-You.

{and he hung up}

Note: As soon as the prerecorded message kicks on saying "final courtesy"… it's scam. Also, there is no top office of Visa / Mastercard, they are two separate companies. If someone says they are from Visa/Mastercard they are lying.

Oh Goody The Marriott Travel Scammers Are Calling...

...you know me, I have to answer...

Me: Hola, como esta?

Scammer: Hi, err, please hold...

{ a minute later}

Scammer: Hi who do I have the privilege of speaking to?

Me: Mi nombre es Roberto.

{they hung up, apparently they only try to scam you if you speak English}

Not more than two hours later I received a call from Hilton with a new travel deal...

Me: Hello.

Scammer: Hi Sir you've been selected to receive a great travel offer from Hilton Hotels

Me: Really?

Scammer: With vacation travel available in Orlando, Cancun, California and more, doesn't that sound wonderful.

Me: Been there, done that.

Scammer: Sir, we are offering a 90% savings off the regular travel prices with food and alcohol all included.

Me: I don't drink…or eat.

Scammer: Wonderful Sir, you will have such a great time.

Me: If you say so.

Scammer: Oh I do, now Sir this fantastic deal is good for up to 4 people, who do you normally travel with…your wife, kids, friends.

Me: Something like that.

Scammer: Well, Sir which one is it.

Me: Which one what?

Scammer: Who do you normally travel with?

Me: Hamsters, lots of them.

{the scammer hung up}

Note: My wife overheard the whole conversation and busted out laughing.

Speaking Of Hamsters

Sir have you ever heard of solar energy?

Me: Is that like from the sun or something?

Scammer: Ha ha, yes it is. Have you ever looked for solar panels?

Me: As in looked do you mean, do I see them on people's roof tops?

Scammer: Well yes, but have you ever considered getting solar panels?

Me: I had a solar calculator once…darn thing never worked inside. And I had solar lights in my garden, the replacement batteries were outrageous in price.

Scammer: Sir…sir, how much do you spend on your electric per month? Less than 100 or more than 100?

Me: The second one.

Scammer: So more than 100? Is it more than 200?

Me: You could say that.

Scammer: Who is your current electric supplier?

Me: HWP!

Scammer: I have never heard of HWP, what does it stand for?

Me: Hamster Wheel Powered – I have like 100 of these furry guys constantly running on wheels to generate my power.

{click}

The Scammer hung up.

Note: These electric rate scammers are notoriously crafty at trying to convince you they are indeed legitimate representatives of some utility company. Unfortunately, all they want to do is rip you off. But if you can waste just a little bit of their time, that's time they aren't conning people. Telling them you have HWP electric gets them every time.

Discover Card Scammers Called...

Is this Robert?

Me: Yup.

Sir, we have reason to believe your card ending in XXXX is compromised and we will need to issue you a new one.

Me: XXXX you say.

Yes Sir.

Me: Okay but that's not the number of my card.

Sir what do you mean?

Me: What part of that's not the number of my card did you not understand?

Sir, that is the number we have on file.

Me: Well, it's wrong.

Sir, could you please read off the last 4 numbers then?

Me: Nope.

Sir, your card starts with 6011 right?

Me: All Discover numbers start with 6011.

Sir, please read the entire number of the card.

Me: Nope.

Sir, we will have no choice but to cancel the card.

Me: Go ahead.

Sir, I don't think you understand the seriousness of this situation.

Me: Please explain.

No Sir just give the card numbers so I can verify your information.

Me: Nope, not happening.

Sir, you are irritating me and not helping your situation.

Me: Good, I have no obligation to help you in your investigation in solving my situation.

Sir?

Me: I'm not helping you.

Well Sir, I'm trying to help you.

Me: Don't want it, didn't ask for it, don't need it.

Sir?

Me: Peddle your scam on someone else.

F-You.
{they hung up}

Note: If any representative of a so-called credit card company calls with the wrong information or presses you into revealing details they should already have on file, most definitely it's a scam.

Ronnie Johnson Is Calling...

To Offer Me A FREE Medical Alert Mobile System Valued At $400

{actually it's a voice automated system using computer AI to guide it along}

Me: Hello.

Ronnie: I need to ask you a set of questions to see if you qualify?

Me: Ask away.

Ronnie: Do you currently use a walker or a cane?

Me: Yes, Johnny Walker with some sugar cane.

Ronnie: That's wonderful. Do you currently live alone?

Me: Hmm, are going to stop over and keep me company?

Ronnie: Based on your answers I believe you qualify.

Me: Oh goody.

Ronnie: Do you understand what we are offering?

Me: A subscription to the scammer of the month club?

Ronnie: It's a medical alert that you use anywhere in the USA and Canada.

Me: How about Mexico?

Ronnie: The system only works in the USA and Canada

Me: How about Europe?

Ronnie: The system only works in the USA and Canada

Me: Well, what if I'm in Australia?

Ronnie: The system only works in the USA and Canada

Me: How about if I'm in Karachi, Pakistan near your call center?

{a slight pause, then I hear a clicking sound followed by a foreign accented male voice who says...}

F-You A-Hole why you waste our time?

Me: So I take it I'm not getting the Free Medical Alert System.

Scammer: {curses at me in Urdu}

Me: Yeah well...same to you.

Scammer: F YOU!
{he finally hung up}

Note: Many scam call centers are switching to computer enhanced voice systems to make it seem safer for consumers. Be careful.

My Buddies From Pakistan Are Calling...

Me: What up dog?

Scammer: Hey buddy.

Me: What's the scoop?

Scammer: Hey buddy.

Me: You said that.

Scammer: Umm, err, aah.

Me: You sound like you lost a chromosome.

Scammer: What?

Me: Did you get dropped on your head during training?

Scammer: Huh?

Me: Were you fed paint chips for lunch?

Scammer: Hey buddy.

Me: How do you say buddy in Pakistani?

Scammer: F You

Me: Nah, but nice try.

Scammer: F You

Me: We've already established that's not the right answer.

{and he hung up}

Note: The fastest way to get scammers off script is to answer the phone without saying "Hi" or "Hello". "What up dog" gets them almost every time.

Not Alex From Apple

Apple iCloud Scammers just called...

"Alert - your Apple iCloud and Apple ID have been compromised, press 1 to speak to a representative".

{me pressing 1}

Hi Sir this is Alex Jones {speaking with a heavy foreign accent that just screams Alex is not his real name} did you know your Apple ID is compromised?

Me: Again?

Not Alex: Sir, then you are aware it's not right.

Me: Well I thought it was fixed last week when another supposed Apple iCloud tech called.

Not Alex: Sir, could you speak up.

Me: I'm speaking just fine, but I would advise you to tell everyone in the call center with you to shut up so you can hear me.

Not Alex: Suck my...

Me: Let me stop you right there...I don't know what kind of weird stuff your call center makes you do, but I doubt it has anything to do with fixing my Apple ID.

Not Alex: F You Mother F'er and Suck My...

Me: Yo Alex if that's your real name...how's the weather in Karachi right now?

{I hear Not Alex tell his call center buddy that my guess in Karachi was correct - and he was instructed to hang up}

Not Alex: F You

Me: Hahahahaha

{He hangs up}

Note: Apple will never call you to tell you your ID was compromised. Oh, and thick foreign accented people rarely have common English names.

Chapter 12

Living Up To The Title

"It's a tough job...but, someone has to do it."

Hey Aren't You The "F-You" Guy?

(a message I received on FB chat from a non-friend)

Me: I'm the what now?

Them: That's what all the scammers and morons say to you after you waste their time and give them sarcastic answers.

Me: Ha, ha, ha...I guess I am then.

Them: Yeah, I love those books.

Me: Awesome, thank you.

Them: You should write another.

Me: Funny you should say that...I'm producing book 3 now.

Them: Awesome, when will it be out?

Me: Probably September.

Them: Why so long?

Me: Well I have other books I'm working on.

Them: You write other books?

Me: Well, yah.

Them: Are they funny.

Me: That depends on how much you've been drinking or how medicated you are I suppose.

Them: So that's a No.

Me: Sure.

Them: Why didn't you just say NO?

{Oh I knew right then how this was going to end}

Me: Oh I don't know, maybe because NO just doesn't sound funny.

Them: F you.

Me: Well at least I'm living up to your title now.

Them: F you.

Me: That's Mr. F You to you.

{he then blocked me}

Note: Somedays the books just write themselves.

Rob Anspach

Chapter 13

The Power Of Being Me

"Fueled by sarcasm...with a touch of grumpy."

What Rob Does Is Not Normal Human Behavior

I Was Exhausted At How People Will Use Any Situation Or Excuse As To Why They Can't Listen Or Pay What Someone Is Charging...

So I took to Facebook to voice my concern.

Me: I'm trying to help as many business owners as possible with their marketing. But they have to be willing to listen. If they are going to tell me how to help them or say how come you won't accept a lesser amount when I told them how much I charge...I will fire them on the spot and keep whatever money they sent me. My patience is wearing thin. Some of you are taking advantage of various situations to not pay what people are worth.

Then the slew of responses happened...

Vivian: Believe me, if I had the money, I wouldn't want anyone but you.

Marc: Welcome to marketing 101, where marketing "just happens," and why would business owners think it happened for a reason other than their own doing.

Shelly: You are invaluable and not just because you are kind and smart... worth 10x.

Baeth: Yes they must be coach-able or adios!

But then...the debate happened!

Manuj: Rob Anspach - I struggled with this for a loooooooong time. When you know too much you want to protect and preach to the masses. From my experience, it is just better to "forget" what you know and meet the client where they are...at least that was my epiphany in last few weeks.

Me: Manuj - it might work for you...not my style.

Manuj: Rob Anspach - yes it is not easy for me either.

Me: Manuj - then don't do it.

Manuj: All I did was to compare my call recordings with people I was brutally honest with and I gave the people what they wanted to hear. The latter group was much more happy and "willing" to listen. So now I can help them truly liberate.

Manuj: Rob Anspach - we all have our own path and our own life experience. I think I can save them, those who want to be saved. So I will continue doing it as long as it feels right. If it stops feeling right - of course I will stop at that moment.

Me: Manuj - one day it will hit you...and you'll say Rob was right. ☺

Manuj: I am sure Rob. I have always honored wisdom over my own experience. Why re-invent the wheel? And what I appreciate about you is brutal honesty and clarity of thought. Very, very valuable. I am definitely going to digest your suggestion and apply to different aspects of my life. Your experience and knowledge is too precious to brush away. I do not take anything you say lightly.... At the same time, I love exploring my own human experience and taking new risks and see what comes out of it. Right now, I am trying to wrap the required medicine in candy so that everyone gets what they think they need but what they actually get is what they TRULY need.

Me: Manuj - you can't please everyone- and no sugar coated pill will make it easier - discover who you want as a client, focus on them exclusively and never accept less.

Manuj: Rob Anspach - great words of wisdom. I am so grateful for you sharing your wisdom so freely and generously. I will definitely take time to ponder upon your advice and how I can incorporate it into my life. thanks so much. How about another podcast episode?

Parthiv: I am watching this conversation between Rob and Manuj. I can see both sides. I too am firm in my price and deliverables, but I have a lot of patience, unlike Rob. Not everyone can behave like Rob. It suits HIS personality. I too am firm on my price and delivery and I too don't want to be taken advantage of, but when I am not making money, I am making friends and I need them both. So Manuj is not out of line feeling startled by Rob's advice. What Rob Anspach does is not normal human behavior. It is a very different business style. I can't just adopt his style just like that.

Me: Parthiv - hah, I've spent 25 years studying human behavior and no one is "normal". But yes I agree how I do things is contrary to what most are taught. Why? Because it works. We as business owners do not have to capitulate to the whims of consumers and do things because that is what they expect. Instead we inform the customer how we operate and if they are acceptable to those terms great. If not, they are free to go elsewhere.

Manuj: Rob Anspach and Parthiv have great points. I think that is what makes entrepreneurship so interesting. I believe it is the best path to self-discovery. We all look at the world differently based on our past experiences. Rob, for instance, I grew up in a small town for the first 20 years of my life. Those were the formative years for my mind. Even if I wanted to - I cannot get rid of some subconscious biases I picked up along the way. The key here to stay flexible. Especially in challenging times like these. Anything I have achieved in my life is by shutting up my inner smartass and learning new paradigms and adapting them to my temperament. So I listen to all the advice - but I only implement it after customizing it for myself :-)

Me: If I shut up my inner smart-ass I wouldn't have written all the books I have nor have attracted awesome clients. In fact, you and I probably wouldn't be friends. See how that works...when you are your authentic self, people gravitate to be near you. They respect you for being who you are. If I suppressed that then I would attract clients I really don't want to deal with and probably wouldn't be an entrepreneur at all.

Note: Both Parthiv and Manuj are good friends whom I respect a great deal. And you can find the interviews I did with them on my E-Heroes Podcast.

Lastly…

Every entrepreneur should have a set a questions they use to interview potential customers, employees and vendors. The list of questions is up to you. But being that I'm not normal in how I do things I will gladly share with you my list…

Questions I'll be asking new clients…

1) Do you have a mental disorder?

2) Do you currently see a therapist?

3) Do you get triggered by feelings?

4) Do you change your mind often?

5) Do you blame others incessantly?

6) Do you demand to be treated like a diva?

7) Do you throw tantrums when not happy?

8) Do you threaten lawsuits when mad?

9) Do you post negative reviews to be vindictive?

10) Have you taken your meds today?

About the Author

Rob is a Certified Digital Marketing Strategist, a Foremost Expert On Specialized SEO, a Serial Author, Podcaster, Speaker and Authority Broadcaster who can help amplify YOU to your audience.

Rob has also produced books for many clients including lawyers, doctors, copywriters, speakers and consultants.

Rob helps companies across the globe generate new revenue and capture online business. And he hates scammers with a passion.

Rob is available to share talks and give interviews.

To learn more about Rob visit **AnspachMedia.com** or call Anspach Media at **(412)267-7224** today.

Resources

THE INTERVIEW SERIES FOR ENTREPRENEURS

Rob Anspach interviews talented entrepreneurs who demonstrate an eagerness to share their experiences, their knowledge and their stories to help others succeed.

Listen to the Rob Anspach's E-Heroes Podcast today.

Available on:

Apple, Google, Himalaya, Stitcher, Spotify, TuneIn

Or

www.AnspachMedia.com

Rob Versus The Scammers

Protecting The World Against Fraud, Nuisance Calls & Downright Phony Scams.

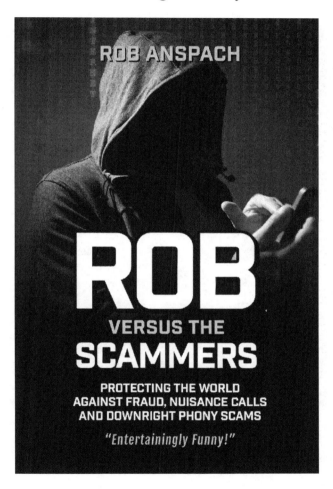

**Available on Amazon in Print & Kindle
or at…
www.RobVersusTheScammers.com**

Rob Versus The Morons

Overcoming Idiotic Customers With Wit, Sarcasm And A Take No Bullshit Attitude

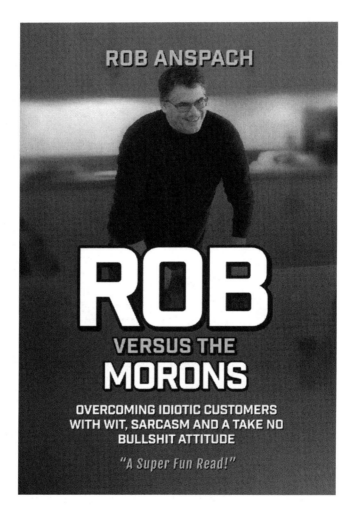

**Available on Amazon in Print & Kindle
or at…
www.RobVersusTheMorons.com**

Other Books By Rob Anspach

Available on Amazon in Print & Kindle.

www.amazon.com/author/robertanspach

Remember to…

Share This Book!

Share it with your friends!

Share it with your colleagues!

Share it with law enforcement!

Share it on social media.

Share it using this hashtag...

#RobVersusHumanity

Made in the USA
Middletown, DE
19 September 2020